BATH

A Little Souvenir

CHRIS ANDREWS PUBLICATIONS

Pulteney Bridge and the weir on the River Avon

BATH

Introduction

Bath is an incredible city. Its wonderful buildings use the local, golden limestone to great effect and any visit will stay long in the memory. It is a World Heritage City and yet is surprisingly small and easily explored.

At its heart lie the hot springs, unique in Britain, and first discovered by the Celts who believed the waters had mystical and healing properties. But it was the skill of the Roman engineers who developed the hot springs. They built a reservoir around the spring and then piped the water to a series of baths which they used for religious, health and relaxation purposes. Beside the baths they constructed a temple to their god Sulis Minerva. You can still see the sacred spring and temple courtyard and these Roman remains are amongst the finest in Europe. When the Roman occupation of Britain declined, the Saxons and then the Normans arrived in Bath. The first major Christian church was built and in medieval times the city, like much of the Cotswolds, built its wealth on wool.

Early morning at the Great Bath   5

6   Wood's Work.....

The Abbey you see today is the third church on this site and was begun in 1499. Its huge windows have earned it the title 'Lantern of the West' but it is the fan vaulting inside that is a must see.

The Georgians developed the city into one of the most fashionable places in Europe. During the early 1700's major redesign cleared a lot of the medieval city in favour of new building, much of which was designed by John Wood, the architect responsible for Queen Square and The Circus. Bath's most famous architectural masterpiece is the Royal Crescent built in the late 1760's by Wood's son, John Wood the Younger.

Fan Vaulting and the Abbey ceiling   7

Royal Crescent

The bold sweep of 30 houses cannot fail to take the breath away as you approach from Brock Street and is one of the best cityscapes in the world. With the elegance of the buildings came a social life which was as famous as that in London. Beau Nash, the Master of Ceremonies, ensured the bathing, promenading, balls and assemblies made Bath the height of fashion and the envy of most cities. It is not surprising then that Bath attracted an extraordinary range of notable people and the brass

10   Spa Waters at The Pump Room   The statue at the Jane Austen Museum

plaques on numerous properties commemorate these visits. Jane Austen was one such visitor and she lived in Bath in the early 1800's. Her novels capture the way of life in Bath and *Northanger Abbey* and *Persuasion* are largely set in the city.

Bath is using its greatest natural gift once again with the opening of the Thermae Bath Spa, a new opportunity to benefit from the health giving properties of the hot waters.

Visitors to Bath will find a lively city with buskers and entertainers, live music, festivals, theatre and exhibitions, as well as architectural variety and history.

The Thermae Bath Spa   11

12   The Avon below Pulteney Bridge

Sham Castle, a folly built in the late 1700's   13

14   The Cross Bath one of the three places where the hot springs emerge

Open-air Rooftop Pool at Thermae Bath Spa - Britain's only natural thermal Spa 15

16   Dawn sun appears to show a statue leaping into the Baths

The Great Bath, centrepiece of The Roman Baths   17

18   Roman statue and flares

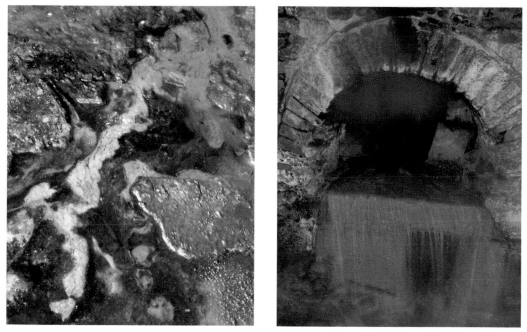

Colourful effects of minerals on a bath floor and on the Roman overflow from The Springs 19

20 Arch that supported the Roman ceiling which covered The Great Bath

Brick 'Pilarii' that facilitated Roman underfloor heating   21

22   The King's Bath

Statue of King Bladud, legendary founder of the city 23

Steam rising from
The Great Bath in
the early morning

Bath is a city of festivals with major arts events taking place throughout the year. The lovely Theatre Royal is one of the leading receiving houses in the country. Its varied programme changes weekly and a night at this beautifully restored theatre is a treat.

The city also has a proud sporting tradition so if rugby, cricket, horseracing or football is your interest it can be found in Bath. And did you know that the University's excellent sports facilities have trained some of our top Olympic athletes. If you want to participate then there's golf or hot air ballooning which has been popular in this area for many years. Viewing the symmetry and design of Bath's streets, parades and crescents is best

done from high above the city. For walkers the choice is endless. Strolling in the city in the age old tradition of promenading is the best way to see Bath. The city is surrounded by the most wonderful countryside and there are many marked footpaths, including the Cotswold Way, the 100 mile footpath that winds its way along the Cotswold escarpment to Chipping Campden.

Sit and watch the world go by from a café, dine in an excellent restaurant, or explore some of the city's superb shops, there is always plenty to do. Bath is a wonderful, vibrant and cosmopolitan city - have fun exploring it for yourself.

The Crystal Palace in Abbey Green 27

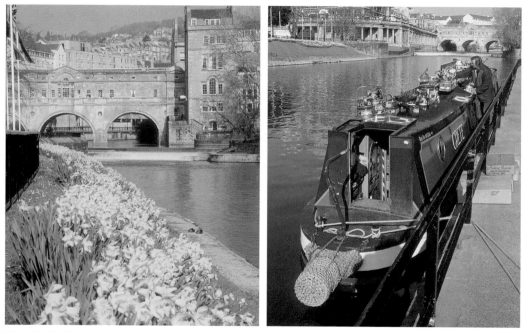

28   Daffodils and the Avon below Pulteney Bridge, the only building in Bath by Robert Adam

Kennet and Avon Canal with St Matthew's Church   29

30   Parade Gardens and St John's Church

Abbey and Baths at dusk   31

32   The City centre and River Avon

Royal Crescent
and The Circus

34   Late evening from Beechen Cliff

36   View from Bathwick

38 Camden Crescent

Bath Abbey, the 'Lantern of the west' 39

The view from Widcombe Hill

Bath was built in the centre of seven hills, which for the Romans had a resonance with their city

42   Passage ways: Entrance to the Hospital of St John and arcading in Bath Street

North Parade
Passage with one of
Bath's oldest
buildings –
Sally Lunn's House

44   Great Pulteney Street with traditional shops

Pulteney Bridge, designed by Robert Adam and completed in 1773, is one of only four bridges in the world with shops across the entire span

46 Gay Street below The Circus

48   Guildhall carvings

Wysteria in Great Pulteney Street   49

50   Abbey Green, a lovely square with original stone sets and a large Plane tree

PRESENTED BY C.GEARY.ESQ.

On the gateway to Royal Victoria Park   51

52   The clock on The Blue Coat School

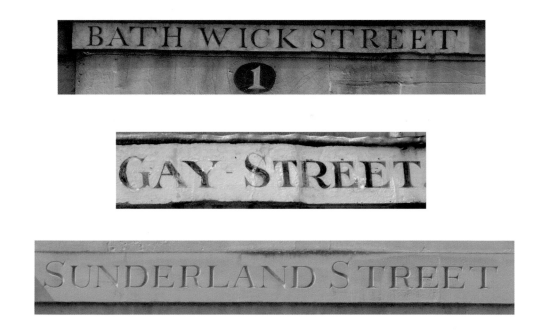

54 Original carved street names dating from the 18th century and other historical reminders ...

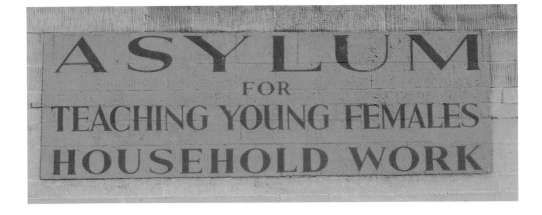

ASYLUM
FOR
TEACHING YOUNG FEMALES
HOUSEHOLD WORK

56　The weir below Pulteney Bridge

58   Floral display at The Abbey and the actors monument in Seven Dials

Riverside walk along the Avon 59

60 Bath is also noted for its parks, Parade Gardens sits right in the centre

Henrietta Park a few minutes walk from Pulteney Bridge 61

62   Procession and musicians at the Bath Music Festival

The Abbey illuminated at the Festival Opening Night

First published 2006, Reprinted 2008, 2010, 2011, updated 2014 by
Chris Andrews Publications Ltd, 15 Curtis Yard, North Hinksey Lane, Oxford, OX2 0LX
Telephone: +44(0)1865 723404 **www.cap-ox.com**
Photos Chris Andrews. Text Jan Hull. © Chris Andrews Publications Ltd. **ISBN 978 1 905385 13 3**

Acknowledgement:
Photographs of The Roman Baths Museum by kind permission of Bath and North East Somerset Council.
Photographs on pages 11 and 15 by kind permission of The Thermae Bath Spa, **www.thermaebathspa.com**
This publication owes much to the ability and knowledge of Jan Hull at Sulis Guides, Bath **www.sulisguides.com**

Front Cover: The Great Bath   Title page: Stone carving above The Great Bath
This page: Detail in Royal Crescent   Back cover: The City from the south